Don't Misunderstand Me

I Love You…Most of the Time!

Relationship Conversation Edition

A humorous look at the mismatch between what we say and what we're really thinking and how it changes over time.

Merrilee Kimble
Jason Myers

Don't Misunderstand Me
I Love You...Most of the Time!
Relationship Conversation Edition
By Merrilee Kimble & Jason Myers

Copyright © 2007 by CleverLivingOnline.com, LLC.

Published by CleverLivingOnline.com, LLC

All rights reserved. No portion of this book may be reproduced or used in any form or by any means – including graphic, electronic or mechanical, including photocopying, recording, taping or information storage and retrieval systems without prior written permission of the publisher except in the case of brief quotations in the context of reviews.

For information write to books@dontmisunderstandme.com

Drawings by Merrilee Kimble

Any similarities to names of actual people, companies, products, mantras or idiotic phraseology mentioned herein are coincidental. Unless otherwise noted, the people, places and events depicted herein are fictitious, and no association with any real person, place or event is intended or should be inferred. So, get over it.

Any similarity between a caricature contained herein and any real person is purely coincidental. This is a work of fiction. Any similarity to any person is purely coincidental. No statement or quotation is an attempt to defame the character of any person on the basis of libel, as the work is FICTIONAL (and NOT an intentionally false statement created with the express purpose of misleading others about the actual character of said person).

ISBN: 978-0-6151-7675-8
First Printing

Introduction

If you're looking for a humor-filled and dare we say, sarcastic or perhaps brutally honest view of what really goes on in a relationship...sit back, relax and read on.

Aw, relationships! They can be the best of times and they can be the worst of times.

At their best, relationships are an amazing, exciting, adventurous, loving and fulfilling thrill ride. At their worst, relationships are a dark and stormy nightmare with no foreseeable means of escape.

Most of the time, though, relationships operate in the middle. A rather happy place where everyday life takes place: work, kids, bills, errands, friends, family, household issues, dining and every once in awhile a few moments to just relax and perhaps have a romantic moment or two.

In any new relationship, even the day to day activities are fun and exciting. It's the honeymoon period for the first couple of years. Filled with discovering wonderful things about each other and the feelings of love and admiration, a new relationship is filled with endless exhilaration and emotion.

Each day you feel as if you are the luckiest person in the world because you met and fell in love with this amazing partner. Your eyes light up when you think of them and your heart beats faster whenever you are near them. Their touch sends a rush of emotions swirling through your body and your every sense is alive with anticipation and desire.

Gradually, you start to notice little things about each other that trigger questions in your mind.

Typically, they are little things that certainly don't call into question the value or worth of the relationship. They are just little oddities or annoyances that are, at first, easily dismissed.

Eventually when you have, let's say, picked your partner's bath towel off the bathroom floor for the fifth or sixth time, you might start to find yourself just a little bit annoyed. You start to question yourself. Did they always do this? Did they do this before and I didn't notice? Why would they do that? Why would they drop the towel on the floor for me to pick up?

As towels on the bathroom floor are added with dishes in the sink, perhaps a lack of helping around the house, frivolous spending, extra time spent with friends – you find yourself in the second stage of a relationship. Typically this stage lasts from years three to six.

At this point, the relationship has its challenges. The conversations are focused less on how cute your partner's ears are and how you just love to nibble them, and more on the endless why questions. Why do you leave your towel on the floor? Why can't you put the dishes in the dishwasher? Why did you spend that much? Why did you stay out so late with your friends?

This part of the relationship is a time of discovery, insecurities, doubt and struggles to determine who is right and who is wrong. The desire to equally be in control, to be needed, to be respected and, of course, to be loved is at the heart of the effort.

As you learn to deal with one another through the challenges, a different and stronger love emerges. You begin to realize that your partner loves you and you love your partner on a very deep and meaningful level. The day to day challenges, the need for control and the need to be needed become less volatile. You develop an appreciation for the love and respect that you have for each other and how it outweighs the challenges.

Now you're reaching the third stage, which is one of balance and perspective. It's called many things: settling, settling down, surrender, acceptance or perhaps happiness. You begin to realize that your partner is whomever he or she is and your energy is better spent on other things rather than trying to get them to pick up their towel off the bathroom floor. Or perhaps you just learn to celebrate the times when they do pick up their towel.

At this stage you can see both sides of your partner. The fantastic attributes that were all you could see in the initial stage of your relationship and the challenges or faults that filled that second stage. The ability to see both gives you balance, humor, humility and deep, committed love.

Throughout all the stages of a relationship, there are the thoughts you share and communicate and those little thoughts that pop up during the conversation that you keep to yourself.

Those thoughts that you keep to yourself are usually a bit more detailed or perhaps edgier than what is actually being spoken. It's all the things you might like to say if your self-respect and the other person's feelings were not as relevant as they actually are.

Let's face it, when you say, "Honey, could you please pick your towel up," you're likely thinking quite a few more things than you are actually saying. The funny thing about those little unspoken thoughts is how they change as a relationship progresses through the stages.

In the following pages we take a look at those thoughts, in each stage. After you read this book, you just might find yourself doing a few double takes! After all, when you take a look at your own thoughts during a conversation you may find yourself wondering what your partner is thinking or meaning as they converse with you!

*"Love asks me no questions,
And gives me endless support..."*

- *Shakespeare*

Casual Conversations

"Wait a second…what did you just say?"

2 | Casual Conversations

Spoken -

"Don't misunderstand me."

Meanings & Thoughts -

Years 0-2:
Oh honey, I must not have said it the right way…I'm sorry.

Years 3-6:
Really? I've said this before, don't you remember?

Years 7+:
Seriously, are you an idiot?

4 | Casual Conversations

Spoken -

"Yep, yep, yep."

Meanings & Thoughts -

Years 0-2:
Oh I know exactly what you mean and that is so true!

Years 3-6:
I know you're talking but can we speed it up a bit?

Years 7+:
I see your lips moving but I have no idea what you're saying.

Spoken -

"Not a chance."

Meanings & Thoughts -

Years 0-2:
Well, maybe! If you nibble on my ear, it would certainly help your chances.

Years 3-6:
What's in it for me? I've been wanting a new....

Years 7+:
Not a chance!

Spoken -

"Calm Down."

Meanings & Thoughts -

Years 0-2:
Are you okay? Are you hurt? Can I help?

Years 3-6:
Good grief, enough with the drama!

Years 7+:
Seriously, you are giving me a headache the size of a small country. I need an aspirin and you better not have taken the last one again. The last time you gave me a headache there wasn't an aspirin in the house.

Spoken -

"Honey!", "Pumpkin!", "Sweetie!"

Meanings & Thoughts -

Years 0-2:
I love you!

Years 3-6:
Hey, could you get over here?

Years 7+:
Ok, here is the list of what I need and what I need you to do.

Spoken -

"Yeah, but…"

Meanings & Thoughts -

Years 0-2:
That's the way you want to do and I want to do it my way. I'll make it worth your while if we do it my way!

Years 3-6:
We always do it your way. Could we once, just once, do it my way?

Years 7+:
It's not going to happen that way. If you want to think it's going to happen that way, feel free. But it's not!

14 | Casual Conversations

Spoken -

"I don't know about that."

Meanings & Thoughts -

Years 0-2:
Oh ok! Whatever you want!

Years 3-6:
That sounds like it might be a really stupid idea. You know, it wouldn't be your first bone-headed idea!

Years 7+:
There is absolutely no chance of that happening.

Spoken -

"It's not you..."

Meanings & Thoughts -

Years 0-2:
Oh it must be me…I'm sorry.

Years 3-6:
Really? Because even though you are saying it's not me, I'm feeling you think it's me.

Years 7+:
Damn right, it's not me!

Casual Conversations

Spoken -

"I can't help you with that right now."

Meanings & Thoughts -

Years 0-2:
Oh now, I feel so bad.

Years 3-6:
Perhaps once I get done with work, kids, bills, cooking, cleaning and grocery shopping, I can get right on that.

Years 7+:
So figure it out for yourself. Good luck!

20 | Casual Conversations

Spoken -

"I think that is a great idea."

Meanings & Thoughts -

Years 0-2:
You are so smart! I am so lucky to have such an amazing person in my life.

Years 3-6:
Especially if it doesn't involve me doing anything to make it happen!

Years 7+:
Wow! I'm shocked.

Casual Conversations

Spoken -

"I need your input and advice."

Meanings & Thoughts -

Years 0-2:
Help me please! I so value what you have to say and you always have such great ideas.

Years 3-6:
You are not going to like the situation that I've gotten into.

Years 7+:
So listen up and pay attention because this is what we are going to do and how we are going to do it.

24 | Casual Conversations

Spoken -

"Good for you!"

Meanings & Thoughts -

Years 0-2:
That is so great. You are such a fantastic person.

Years 3-6:
It's about time and I'm proud of you.

Years 7+:
I'm shocked!

Spoken -

"That's so funny!"
"That's so hilarious!"

Meanings & Thoughts -

Years 0-2:
You are just the funniest person I have ever met. You make me laugh all the time. You are so wonderful.

Years 3-6:
You're cute. "Funny" is questionable but you're cute.

Years 7+:
Are you making fun of me?

Spoken -

"I need your help."

Meanings & Thoughts -

Years 0-2:
I hate to ask you for a favor. You are always so generous and I don't want to take advantage of that.

Years 3-6:
I helped you at least three times this month so I think it's only fair that you help me this one time.

Years 7+:
You owe me and it's time to pay up.

Spoken -

"Shit if I know…"

Meanings & Thoughts -

Years 0-2:
Really…I haven't a clue.

Years 3-6:
How many times and ways are you going to ask me the same thing?

Years 7+:
You figure it out!

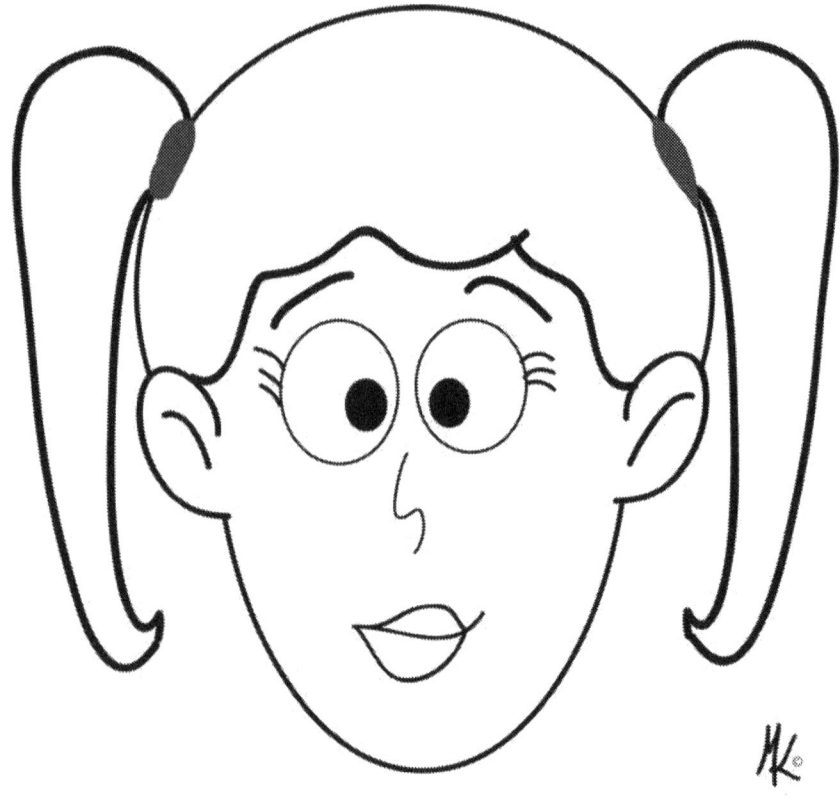

Spoken -

"I love you."

Meanings & Thoughts -

Years 0-2:
You are the sun, the moon and the stars. I'm so lucky.

Years 3-6:
Do you love me?

Years 7+:
Despite your faults!

34 | Casual Conversations

Spoken -

"I'm so glad to have you in my life."

Meanings & Thoughts -

Years 0-2:
I'm just the luckiest person ever.

Years 3-6:
I'm thinking that I just might keep you around!

Years 7+:
If I had to manage all this on my own…good grief, there is no way!

36 | Casual Conversations

Spoken -

"Be careful!"

Meanings & Thoughts -

Years 0-2:
I don't know what I would do without you.

Years 3-6:
I'm going to kick your ass if you get hurt.

Years 7+:
Is your life insurance current?

Spoken -

"You know I'm sorry."

Meanings & Thoughts -

Years 0-2:
I never meant to hurt you. I feel so bad. Please forgive me!

Years 3-6:
I'm not sure why I always have to say it.

Years 7+:
So get over it!

Spoken -

"What were you doing with her/him?"

Meanings & Thoughts -

Years 0-2:
You are not interested in them are you? Am I doing something wrong?

Years 3-6:
I'm going to kick your butt. Do I need to kick her/his butt too?

Years 7+:
This is going to cost you…big!

42 | Casual Conversations

Spoken -

"As far as I'm concerned, you are the only one for me."

Meanings & Thoughts -

Years 0-2:
I love you so deeply and completely.

Years 3-6:
Am I the only one for you?

Years 7+:
Do you know how long it would take me to train someone else?

Spoken -

"I don't feel well."

Meanings & Thoughts -

Years 0-2:
Will you hold me and take care of me until I feel better?

Years 3-6:
Do you care? Will you help me?

Years 7+:
I need some alone time!

Spoken -

"What's for dinner?"

Meanings & Thoughts -

Years 0-2:
How can I help? Shall we go out?

Years 3-6:
You did take care of dinner, didn't you?

Years 7+:
I hope it's not your pot roast. Good grief that always tastes so bad.

Spoken -

"Did you hear me?"

Meanings & Thoughts -

Years 0-2:
I'm sorry honey, should I repeat that?

Years 3-6:
Was I speaking a different language?

Years 7+:
HELLO!

Spoken -

"I'm concerned about you. Is there anything I can do to help?"

Meanings & Thoughts -

Years 0-2:
I hope you are ok. I want to do anything I can to help.

Years 3-6:
And we need to make this snappy because my schedule is packed today.

Years 7+:
Good grief. What is going on with you?

52 | Casual Conversations

Spoken -

"W-h-a-t?"

Meanings & Thoughts -

Years 0-2:
Did I hear that correctly, honey? Could you repeat that?

Years 3-6:
Are you kidding me?

Years 7+:
What the hell is wrong with you?

Spoken -

"Now listen."

Meanings & Thoughts -

Years 0-2:
I'm serious now, honey-bear!

Years 3-6:
Is there a magical number of times that I need to say this so it will register?

Years 7+:
This is the way it's going to be!

Spoken -

"I believe in you."

Meanings & Thoughts -

Years 0-2:
You are just the most amazing person ever. I know you can do anything. You are just magic in my heart!

Years 3-6:
Do you know that?

Years 7+:
Now go get it done.

Spoken -

"Are you mad at me?"

Meanings & Thoughts -

Years 0-2:
I'm sorry honey, should I repeat that?

Years 3-6:
What did I do know?

Years 7+:
Again?

Casual Conversations

Spoken -

"How was your day?"

Meanings & Thoughts -

Years 0-2:
I hope it was as wonderful as you.

Years 3-6:
Will I be getting lucky tonight?

Years 7+:
Hmmm…I've got to remember to pay the bills tonight and I think that new show is on TV…excellent!

Romantic Conversations

"Ah, I feel so inspired, but wait a minute…"

Spoken -

"You certainly look fantastic!"

Meanings & Thoughts -

Years 0-2:
Wow! You're a hottie! Lucky me!

Years 3-6:
How about a quickie? We've got a few minutes.

Years 7+:
What's this all about?

"Come on over here and sit next to me."

Meanings & Thoughts -

Years 0-2:
I want to always be right beside you. I just can't get enough of you.

Years 3-6:
How about a quickie? We've got a few minutes.

Years 7+:
I love you!

Spoken -

"I like it when you…"

Meanings & Thoughts -

Years 0-2:
You are so irresistible. I just think about you and my temperature rises.

Years 3-6:
Do you remember when you used to…?

Years 7+:
Though I can't remember when that last happened.

70 | Romantic Conversations

Spoken -

"Not tonight honey, I have a headache."

Meanings & Thoughts -

Years 0-2:
Could you bring me an aspirin and rub my temples?

Years 3-6:
I am just not in the mood. My pillow is calling me.

Years 7+:
Check back next week!

72 | Romantic Conversations

Spoken -

"Are you open to something new?"

Meanings & Thoughts -

Years 0-2:
I can't wait! I love how open and sexy you are.

Years 3-6:
Not that our "routine" isn't fulfilling and well, routine, but perhaps we could just change things around one time? Oh please?

Years 7+:
No, it does not involve the remote control for the TV!

Romantic Conversations

Spoken -

"Do you want to head to the bedroom?"

Meanings & Thoughts -

Years 0-2:
Or the dining room, or the kitchen table or the shower…

Years 3-6:
How about a quickie? We've got a few minutes.

Years 7+:
I think I'll be asleep before my head hits the pillow!

76 | Romantic Conversations

Spoken -

"Let's snuggle."

Meanings & Thoughts -

Years 0-2:
I love snuggling with you. The smell of your hair and the touch of your hands make me weak in the knees.

Years 3-6:
I am way too tired for sex. Let's just snuggle so I can fall asleep.

Years 7+:
I'm freezing! Maybe you can warm me up.

Spoken -

"Have I told you lately how much I love you?"

Meanings & Thoughts -

Years 0-2:
I'm going to tell you every single day just how much I love you.

Years 3-6:
How about a quickie? We've got a few minutes.

Years 7+:
I'm pretty sure I've mentioned it recently. Hmmm…well I can't think of when but I'm sure I have.

80 | Romantic Conversations

Spoken -

"You know, I like it when you..."

Meanings & Thoughts -

Years 0-2:
You are so irresistible! I just can't get you off my mind.

Years 3-6:
Do you remember the last time you…?

Years 7+:
Take out the trash. Do the laundry. I really like it when you do that too!

Romantic Conversations

Spoken -

"On a scale of 1 to 5, you're a 12!"

Meanings & Thoughts -

Years 0-2:
My luscious little love-bunny.

Years 3-6:
How about a quickie? We've got a few minutes.

Years 7+:
Now, can we do what I want to do for a change?

Romantic Conversations

Spoken -

"Let's take a long-weekend vacation."

Meanings & Thoughts -

Years 0-2:
The beach, the balcony…all kinds of new places where we can….

Years 3-6:
I'm dying to use my new clubs. I could play a round each day. Perfect!

Years 7+:
We'll take the kids and the dog and we can all stay in one room.

86 | Romantic Conversations

Spoken -

"I had the most amazing dream about you…"

Meanings & Thoughts -

Years 0-2:
You naughty-sexy man, you!

Years 3-6:
You cleaned the house, picked up the dry cleaning, paid the bills, took out the garbage, finished the honey-do list and prepared a romantic dinner! And then I woke up!

Years 7+:
Ok, it was actually that guy from that new TV show but hey, it could have been you…sort of.

88 | Romantic Conversations

Spoken -

"I want you!"

Meanings & Thoughts -

Years 0-2:
You make my heart race and knees weak when I just think about being with you.

Years 3-6:
…to do whatever I say!

Years 7+:
…to do the laundry and pick up your clothes in the bathroom. Perhaps clean the garage too!

90 | Romantic Conversations

Spoken -

"I need you!"

Meanings & Thoughts -

Years 0-2:
Whenever I'm away from you, all I can do is think about the next time I'll see you again.

Years 3-6:
To let me spend money on…. You know how happy it would make me! After all, when I'm happy, we're happy!

Years 7+:
To finish your to-do list. Is it really too much to ask?

Spoken -

"That feels so good!"

Meanings & Thoughts -

Years 0-2:
You are just the most amazing person that ever walked the planet.

Years 3-6:
Ok, what do you want?

Years 7+:
Who knew you still had it in you. Wow, go tiger!
!

94 | Romantic Conversations

Spoken -

"You're really pushing my buttons!"

Meanings & Thoughts -

Years 0-2:
And I certainly hope you don't stop because you push just the right buttons to turn me on.

Years 3-6:
It would be great if you realized that I have more buttons, but that doesn't seem to be happening.

Years 7+:
You really know how to piss me off, don't you!

Spoken -

"I'm so glad we are together and that we trust one another."

Meanings & Thoughts -

Years 0-2:
We are such a perfect match; I don't know how I got so lucky.

Years 3-6:
I can trust you, can't I?

Years 7+:
Jen and Bob just broke up because it turned out that he was a lying and cheating bum. If you do anything like that I'm going to kick your ass.

Spoken –

"Let me give you a nice relaxing massage."

Meanings & Thoughts -

Years 0-2:
Then I'll nibble on your ears and kiss your neck and….

Years 3-6:
I need a wee bit of a favor and you being in a nice relaxed place will certainly increase my odds of getting you to do what I want.

Years 7+:
Because when you hear what I did, you won't be relaxed again for a good long time.

Spoken -

"I just want to gaze into your eyes."

Meanings & Thoughts -

Years 0-2:
Your eyes are so beautiful. The little flecks that reflect light like the gentle flicker of the flame of a candle. You are so remarkable.

Years 3-6:
Oh prince charming, I want you to pick me up in your arms and whisk me away to the candlelit bedroom and make love to me. Or you could just put the remote control down!

Years 7+:
Have you been drinking or something?

Spoken -

"I love the way you look."

Meanings & Thoughts -

Years 0-2:
And the way you smell and the way you smile and the way you talk. You are perfect!

Years 3-6:
Do you love the way I look?

Years 7+:
Wow! What I wouldn't give to see you look this way more often!

104 | Romantic Conversations

Spoken -

"I love everything about you."

Meanings & Thoughts -

Years 0-2:
You just make my heart beat faster every time I see you or think about you.

Years 3-6:
Do you love everything about me?

Years 7+:
Now let's focus on what I want!

106 | Romantic Conversations

Spoken -

"You're my big strong lover."

Meanings & Thoughts -

Years 0-2:
You satisfy me in every way possible and in so many ways I didn't even know were possible.

Years 3-6:
How about a quickie? I've got a few minutes!

Years 7+:
And I need some help re-arranging the living room furniture!

Romantic Conversations

Spoken -

"I'm on cloud 9 whenever I'm with you."

Meanings & Thoughts -

Years 0-2:
I'm so very lucky and I love you so very much.

Years 3-6:
Are you on cloud 9 whenever you are with me? I don't just mean in the bedroom, I mean all the time!

Years 7+:
I have an amazing imagination!

110 | Romantic Conversations

Spoken -

"You mean the world to me."

Meanings & Thoughts -

Years 0-2:
I can't imagine my life without you and I can't even remember what my life was like before you.

Years 3-6:
But I certainly wonder how much I mean to you.

Years 7+:
Ok, I'm sorry. Now let's get back to doing what I need!

Spoken -

"Sweetheart!"

Meanings & Thoughts -

Years 0-2:
Honey Bunny! Lover Pie! Smooches! Pumpkin!

Years 3-6:
Wow, you surprised me!

Years 7+:
What did you do?

Spoken -

"I love watching you sleep"

Meanings & Thoughts -

Years 0-2:
I love the way you snore. You're so adorable.

Years 3-6:
I do a lot of watching you sleep since you so often keep me awake with your snoring!

Years 7+:
As I grab my pillow and blanket and head to couch to escape your non-stop snoring.

Spoken -

"Our love keeps growing stronger."

Meanings & Thoughts -

Years 0-2:
With every passing second, I love you even more!

Years 3-6:
Like the scent of your socks that I found stuffed into the couch yesterday.

Years 7+:
Who else is going to put with me? Come to think of it, who else is going to put up with you?

Those Fighting Words!

"I can't believe you just…"

Those Fighting Words!

Spoken -

"Why can't you remember...?"

Meanings & Thoughts -

Years 0-2:
I'll help you any way I can. Is there something I can do to help you remember?

Years 3-6:
For the love of potato chips, how many times do I have to say it?

Years 7+:
Do I need to tattoo it on your forehead so you'll remember?

Spoken -

"What were you thinking?"

Meanings & Thoughts -

Years 0-2:
I love you so much and I'm so worried about you!

Years 3-6:
You have truly lost your marbles, haven't you?

Years 7+:
Or should I ask, "what were you thinking with?"

124 | Those Fighting Words!

Spoken -

"Do you think I'm stupid?"

Meanings & Thoughts -

Years 0-2:
Because I would feel so bad if you do, pumpkin! I think the world of you and I hope you think the world of me too.

Years 3-6:
There is only one right answer here!

Years 7+:
Oh, never mind! Don't even answer that!

Those Fighting Words!

Spoken -

"You're making me mad..."

Meanings & Thoughts -

Years 0-2:
I'm feeling confused. Why would my honey bunny do this? Oh my God, is the relationship over?

Years 3-6:
What on earth is wrong with you? You never used to be like this!

Years 7+:
And you know what comes next when you make me mad…

Spoken -

"Why can't we do what I want to do?"

Meanings & Thoughts -

Years 0-2:
You know I'll make it worth your while later on, my honey-bunny!

Years 3-6:
Your idea is stupid and my idea is right. It's a clear choice.

Years 7+:
Why am I asking, I know it's your way or the highway.

Spoken -

"You hurt my feelings!"

Meanings & Thoughts -

Years 0-2:
How could you hurt my feelings? You're my pooky bear and my pooky bear wouldn't hurt my feelings. You couldn't have meant it – what am I thinking?

Years 3-6:
Have you always been this evil and I just haven't noticed? You haven't been like this before and you better have a good explanation.

Years 7+:
You piece of shit!

Those Fighting Words!

Spoken -

"What's wrong with you?"

Meanings & Thoughts -

Years 0-2:
Are you not feeling well? Did you have a bad day? Is there something I can do to make you feel better?

Years 3-6:
You are working my very last nerve!

Years 7+:
Because if there isn't something wrong with you now, there will be when I get done with you!

134 | Those Fighting Words!

Spoken -

"I'll get right on that."

Meanings & Thoughts -

Years 0-2:
I had a few things planned but I can re-arrange my schedule, no problem.

Years 3-6:
When pigs turn purple and start to ride horses in the Kentucky Derby. Moron!

Years 7+:
Whatever! I'll get to it, when I get to it.

Spoken -

"Could you possibly help with..."

Meanings & Thoughts -

Years 0-2:
I would so appreciate your help and I will certainly help you whenever you need anything. I love you.

Years 3-6:
Seriously, it's not crossing your mind to offer to help? Why do I have to ask for your help? Why?

Years 7+:
I mean really, would it kill you? From the look on your face you think it will kill you but really!

Spoken -

"When is the last time you remembered to..."

Meanings & Thoughts -

Years 0-2:
Because I can help you however I can. I'm always happy to help you!

Years 3-6:
Do you even remember how? Perhaps youl need me to provide an instruction manual?

Years 7+:
Do these things really never cross your mind? They used to cross your mind. Why don't they anymore? Maybe if I danced around the house naked it would cross your mind?

140 | Those Fighting Words!

Spoken -

"You're not doing it right!"

Meanings & Thoughts -

Years 0-2:
I don't understand, honey bunny.

Years 3-6:
Good grief! What is wrong with you? Have you always been like this or did you knock your head into something and lose a few cells?

Years 7+:
Moron!

"Love is a promise, love is a souvenir, once given, never forgotten, never let it disappear."

- *John Lennon*

We hope you enjoyed a lot of good laughs!

Relationships are an endless source of every human emotion possible. From laughter to tears, love to loathing, compassion to selfishness, a relationship is like a merry-go-round with different scenery appearing with every pass. However, the greatest part of any relationship is the laughter, fun and amazing feeling of freedom you both share when your hearts are full of love. It's funny how relationships age and the more you hold onto the humor and amusement the more entertaining it can be!

Do you have favorite meanings and interpretations of everyday relationship conversations that you want to share?

Use the following pages to jot down your favorites and come to our website to post your favorites. Check out our latest books while you're there.

www.dontmisunderstandme.com

Thank you –
Merrilee & Jason

My Favorite Meanings of Relationship Conversation: NOTES

1. Phrase: _____

_____

Meanings: _____

_____

_____

2. Phrase: _____

_____

Meanings: _____

_____

_____

3. Phrase: _____

_____

Meanings: _____

_____

_____

4. Phrase: _____
   _____

   Meanings: _____
   _____
   _____

5. Phrase: _____
   _____

   Meanings: _____
   _____
   _____

6. Phrase: _____
   _____

   Meanings: _____
   _____
   _____

www.ingramcontent.com/pod-product-compliance
Lightning Source LLC
Chambersburg PA
CBHW021004090426
42738CB00007B/641